Medicine for My Big Brother

Writers of the Round Table Press
PO Box 511
Highland Park, IL 60035

Illustration	NATHAN LUETH
Publisher	COREY MICHAEL BLAKE
Executive Editor	KATIE GUTIERREZ
Post Production	SUNNY DIMARTINO
President	KRISTIN WESTBERG
Facts Keeper	MIKE WINICOUR
Cover Design	NATHAN LUETH, SUNNY DIMARTINO
Interior Design and Layout	SUNNY DIMARTINO
Proofreading	JONATHAN HIERHOLZER, CHRISTIAN PANNECK
Digital Publishing	SUNNY DIMARTINO

Printed in the United States of America

First Edition: July 2016
10 9 8 7 6 5 4 3 2 1

Library of Congress Cataloging-in-Publication Data
Antonow, Agata
Medicine for my big brother: a comic book about autism, medication,
and brotherly love / Agata Antonow with James G. Balestrieri, Jeff Krukar,
Nicolette Weisensel, and Katie Gutierrez.—1st ed. p. cm.
Print ISBN: 978-1-939418-83-8   Digital ISBN: 978-1-939418-84-5
Library of Congress Control Number: 2016947223
Number 16 in the series: The ORP Library
The ORP Library: Medicine for My Big Brother

RTC Publishing is an imprint of Writers of the Round Table, Inc.
Writers of the Round Table Press and the RTC Publishing logo
are trademarks of Writers of the Round Table, Inc.

Medicine for My Big Brother

A COMIC BOOK ABOUT AUTISM, MEDICATION, AND BROTHERLY LOVE

THE ORP LIBRARY

ILLUSTRATED BY
NATHAN LUETH

WRITTEN BY
AGATA ANTONOW

WITH
JAMES G. BALESTRIERI
JEFF KRUKAR, PH.D.
NICOLETTE WEISENSEL, M.D.
KATIE GUTIERREZ

Introduction

I have led Oconomowoc Residential Programs (ORP) for over thirty years. We're a family of companies offering specialized services and care for children, adolescents, and adults with disabilities. Too often, when parents of children with disabilities try to find funding for programs like ours, they are bombarded by red tape, conflicting information, or no information at all, so they struggle blindly for years to secure an appropriate education. Meanwhile, home life, and the child's wellbeing, suffers. In cases when parents and caretakers have exhausted their options—and their hope—ORP is here to help. We felt it was time to offer parents a new, unexpected tool to fight back: stories that educate, empower, and inspire.

The original idea was to create a library of comic books that could empower families with information to reclaim their rights. We wanted to give parents and caretakers the information they need to advocate for themselves, as well as provide educators and therapists with a therapeutic tool. And, of course, we wanted to reach the children—to offer them a visual representation of their journey that would show that they aren't alone, nor are they wrong or "bad" for their differences.

What we found in the process of writing original stories for the comics is that these journeys are too long, too complex, to be contained within a standard comic. So what we are now creating is an ORP library of disabilities books—traditional books geared toward parents, caretakers, educators, and therapists, *and* comic books like this one that portray the world through the eyes of children with disabilities. Both styles of books share what we have learned while advocating for families over the years while also honestly highlighting their emotional journeys.

In an ideal situation, this companion children's book will be used therapeutically, to communicate directly with these amazing children, and to help support the work ORP and companies like ours are doing. These books are the best I have to offer and if they even help a handful of people the effort will have been worth it.

Sincerely,

Jim Balestrieri
CEO, Oconomowoc Residential Programs

A Note About This Book

Autism spectrum disorder (ASD) is a complex condition that affects children in different ways. In children and adolescents, just as in adults, a lack of appropriate therapeutic and educational intervention can result in both short-term and long-term consequences. Sometimes it is helpful to incorporate psychotropic medication, which can effectively influence brain processes that are associated with emotion regulation and behavior. The following story illustrates the social, emotional, and behavioral difficulties that can occur for a child with ASD and his or her entire family. In this story, the sibling of a child with ASD, Justin, describes his varied emotions about his big brother, Max, and the family's journey to renewed hope with the addition of psychotropic medication to his therapeutic plan.

I LIVE WITH MY MOM, DAD, AND BIG BROTHER, MAX. WHEN I WAS LITTLE, MY PARENTS TOLD ME MAX HAD SOMETHING CALLED AUTISM. IT MEANS MAX IS DIFFERENT FROM MY PARENTS AND ME.

IT'S HARD FOR HIM TO EXPLAIN HOW HE FEELS AND WHAT HE WANTS, SO SOMETIMES HE GETS MAD AND FRUSTRATED—AND WHEN HE DOES, WATCH OUT!

MY PARENTS TRY TO HELP HIM BY GIVING HIM VITAMINS AND HEALTHY FOOD EVERY DAY.

TODAY, MAX DOESN'T WANT TO TAKE HIS VITAMINS. HE LOOKS ANGRY!

MOM AND DAD WANT MAX TO TAKE
HIS VITAMINS, BUT HE WANTS PIZZA.
WHEN MAX IS UPSET, I SOMETIMES
FEEL SCARED.

WE GET TO EAT PIZZA AND MAX TAKES HIS VITAMINS. DAD HELPS HIM GET CALM BY STANDING BEHIND MAX AND PUSHING DOWN ON HIS SHOULDERS AND HELPING HIM BREATHE DEEPLY.

WHEN THAT HAPPENS, I STAY QUIET AND DON'T MOVE. MOVING AROUND AND MAKING LOUD NOISES MAKE MAX ANGRY, SO I REMEMBER TO BE QUIET.

MOM AND DAD TALK ABOUT MAX AND MEDICINE A LOT. DAD WANTS TO HELP MAX WITH VITAMINS AND HEALTHY FOODS. MOM THINKS MAX NEEDS REAL MEDICINE FROM A DOCTOR. DAD IS WORRIED THAT MEDICINE FROM THE DOCTOR WILL MAKE MAX WORSE.

WE NEED TO TAKE MAX IN TO SEE HIS PEDIATRICIAN. THE VITAMINS ALONE JUST AREN'T WORKING.

WE AGREED THAT WE WOULD GO THE NATURAL ROUTE. DO YOU REALLY WANT TO MEDICATE OUR SON?

MOM AND DAD TAKE MAX TO THE DOCTOR AND HE GETS A NEW BOTTLE OF PILLS. HE HAS TO TAKE THEM EVERY DAY.

IT'S IMPORTANT I DON'T PLAY WITH THE PILLS AND THAT MOM GETS TO HAND THEM OUT. THEY ARE NOT TOYS. THEY ARE NOT CANDY. MEDICINE CAN MAKE MAX FEEL BETTER, BUT IF I TAKE THE SAME PILLS, THEY WON'T MAKE ME FEEL BETTER. MOM SAID THEY CAN MAKE ME SICK.

WHEN I CAME HOME FROM SCHOOL TODAY, MAX HAD A BIG BANDAGE ON HIS FACE. MOM TOLD ME MAX GOT UPSET AT SCHOOL AND HURT HIS HEAD. I'M SURPRISED, BECAUSE HE HASN'T DONE THAT IN A LONG TIME.

I ASK MAX IF HE WANTS TO PLAY A VIDEO
GAME WITH ME. HE'S GOOD AT VIDEO GAMES
AND I LIKE IT WHEN WE PLAY TOGETHER.

I START THE GAME ANYWAY. IT'S MY FAVORITE GAME TO PLAY WHEN I DON'T HAVE HOMEWORK.

AT FIRST, I PLAY REALLY QUIETLY
SO MAX DOESN'T GET UPSET. BUT
THEN I WIN! IT'S SO EXCITING I
ACCIDENTALLY JUMP UP AND
SHOUT. I DON'T MEAN TO DO IT.
IT JUST HAPPENS!

MAX STARTS TO YELL. HIS YELLS GET LOUDER AND LOUDER AND LOUDER UNTIL I WANT TO CLAP MY HANDS OVER MY EARS. I FEEL REALLY BAD THAT I STARTLED HIM, EVEN IF IT WAS AN ACCIDENT.

MOM AND DAD COME RUNNING IN TO HELP AND DAD HOLDS MAX TIGHT.

THIS DEEP PRESSURE SOMETIMES HELPS MAX CALM DOWN. TODAY IT DOES. EVERYTHING IN THE HOUSE GOES QUIET.

I TRY TO BE GOOD AND NOT CRY. BUT MY EYES GET ITCHIER AND ITCHIER. I DON'T EVEN FEEL HAPPY I WON MY GAME. MY THROAT FEELS FUNNY AND MY EYES BURN. I CAN'T HELP IT. I DO START TO CRY.

I KNOW EMOTIONS ARE HARD FOR MAX.
HE HAS A HARD TIME CONTROLLING
HOW HE FEELS AND HE GETS UPSET
EASILY. BUT SOMETIMES I GET UPSET,
TOO. I GET SAD.

I WISH MAX AND I COULD HANG OUT
AND PLAY, EVEN MAKE LOTS OF NOISE.
I WISH MOM AND DAD DIDN'T LOOK
WORRIED ALL THE TIME.

MOM EXPLAINS THAT MAX'S MEDICINE HAS SIDE EFFECTS, THE WAY AN ANTIBIOTIC SOMETIMES UPSETS MY TUMMY. ONLY MAX'S MEDICINE IS DIFFERENT THAN ANTIBIOTICS, SO THE SIDE EFFECTS ARE DIFFERENT, TOO. MOM SAYS SHE'S GOING TO TAKE MAX BACK TO THE DOCTOR. DAD DOESN'T SAY ANYTHING. I THINK HE MIGHT BE MAD.

MAX IS AT THE DOCTOR WITH MOM AND DAD. WHILE THEY'RE AWAY, I STAY AT HOME WITH A NEW BABYSITTER. I GET TO PLAY MY VIDEO GAMES AS LOUD AS I WANT.

IT'S PRETTY COOL, BUT I AM A LITTLE LONELY.

WHEN MOM, DAD, AND MAX COME HOME, THEY HAVE A LITTLE WHITE PAPER BAG WITH A SMALL BOTTLE IN IT. MOM SHOWS ME THE PILLS FOR MAX.

THEY ARE SHINY AND SHE KEEPS THEM IN THE TOP OF THE KITCHEN CUPBOARD. SHE TELLS ME TO NEVER TOUCH THEM. THEY ARE NOT CANDY. THEY ARE NOT TOYS. THEY WILL MAKE MAX FEEL BETTER BUT THEY COULD MAKE ME SICK.

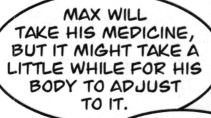

DAD TELLS ME ABOUT THE MEDICINE.
HE SAYS THAT EVERYBODY'S BRAIN IS
LIKE A COMPUTER WITH LOTS OF
PROGRAMS THAT HELP US TO EAT,
TALK TO PEOPLE, PLAY GAMES, AND GO
TO SCHOOL. BUT MAX'S BRAIN HAS
PROGRAMS THAT WORK DIFFERENTLY.

IT MAKES IT HARD FOR MAX TO MAKE
FRIENDS. IT MAKES IT HARD FOR MAX TO TELL
US WHAT HE WANTS OR WHEN HE GETS SAD
OR ANGRY OR WORRIED. IT MAKES IT HARD
FOR MAX WHEN HE HEARS LOUD SOUNDS.

SOMETIMES MEDICINE CAN BE VERY HELPFUL, DAD SAYS. DOCTORS CAN GIVE MAX MEDICINE TO MAKE HIS BRAIN WORK A LITTLE DIFFERENTLY. IT COULD HELP HIM GET LESS UPSET, ESPECIALLY LIKE HE DOES WHEN THINGS CHANGE, LIKE YESTERDAY WHEN IT WAS RAINING AND MOM SAID WE COULDN'T GO OUTSIDE.

BUT IT CAN TAKE TIME FOR THE DOCTORS TO FIGURE OUT THE KIND OF MEDICINE AND HOW MUCH HE NEEDS. EVERYONE'S BODY IS DIFFERENT.

I WISH I COULD UNDERSTAND HOW THE COMPUTER IN MAX'S BRAIN WORKS. THEN MAYBE WE COULD DO MORE FUN STUFF LIKE PLAY VIDEO GAMES TOGETHER WITHOUT HIM GETTING UPSET WHEN HE LOSES.

MAX WOULD BE HAPPY AND I WOULD BE HAPPY, TOO.

MAX TAKES HIS MEDICATION EVERY DAY
NOW. AT FIRST I THINK HE IS BETTER. HE
IS MORE QUIET AND CALM. HE'S ALSO
EATING MORE. THEN HE CAN'T FIT IN HIS
FAVORITE T-SHIRT. SOMETIMES, HE RUBS
HIS STOMACH A LITTLE, LIKE IT HURTS.

HE DOESN'T SAY MUCH TO ME, AND HAS A
HARD TIME FALLING ASLEEP. MOM AND DAD
HAVE TO TAKE TURNS TRYING TO PUT HIM
BACK TO BED IN THE MIDDLE OF THE NIGHT
BECAUSE HE ALWAYS TRIES TO GO INTO
THEIR ROOM. WE'RE ALL TIRED.

I GET OUT THE BUTTER KNIFE AND THE PEANUT BUTTER. MAX LOOKS A BIT UPSET BECAUSE MOM MAKES THE TOAST EVERY DAY. BUT HE WATCHES AND WAITS FOR THE TOAST.

I DROP THE KNIFE. IT'S AN ACCIDENT. IT MAKES A BIG NOISE AND MAX PUTS HIS HANDS OVER HIS EARS. HE STARTS TO LOOK MAD.

I'M TIRED AND I WANT MY TOAST, BUT I GET MAD, TOO. I'M JUST TRYING TO HELP! I'M MAKING MAX'S TOAST FIRST AND TRYING TO BE A GOOD BROTHER!

BE QUIET! MOM'S SLEEPING!

I YELL AT MAX. I DON'T MEAN TO, BUT I'M MAD. I LOVE HIM, BUT RIGHT NOW I DON'T LIKE HIM VERY MUCH.

MAX GETS SO MAD HE PUSHES ME OVER AND PUTS HIS HANDS ON MY NECK. IT HURTS AND I CAN'T BREATHE.

I GET REALLY SCARED AND TRY TO PUSH HIM AWAY, BUT HE'S A LOT BIGGER THAN ME.

MAX HITS MOM WHEN SHE TAKES HIS ARM. SHE COVERS HER FACE AND I START TO CRY. I'M SCARED OF WHAT'S GOING TO HAPPEN NEXT.

I RUB MY THROAT. IT HURTS LIKE IT DOES
WHEN I HAVE A BAD SORE THROAT.
I DON'T UNDERSTAND WHY MAX WOULD
TRY TO HURT ME LIKE THAT BECAUSE BIG
BROTHERS AREN'T SUPPOSED TO DO THAT.
I'M CRYING REALLY HARD.

MOM TELLS ME TO RUN. MAX IS STILL SHOUTING. I STILL HURT AND MY HEART IS BEATING VERY, VERY FAST.

A POLICE OFFICER ARRIVES AND THEN AN AMBULANCE. A WOMAN FROM THE AMBULANCE GIVES MAX A TYPE OF MEDICINE IN A NEEDLE. IT MAKES MAX FALL ASLEEP RIGHT AWAY.

WE'RE TAKING HIM TO RIDGEVIEW HOSPITAL.

I STAY AT HOME WITH A DIFFERENT
BABYSITTER WHILE MOM AND DAD GO
TO THE HOSPITAL TO SEE MAX.

I WAIT AND WAIT BY THE WINDOW. IT GETS
DARK OUTSIDE AND I WAIT SOME MORE.
I'M NERVOUS AND I DON'T WANT TO EAT.

MOM AND DAD COME HOME. THEY LOOK REALLY TIRED. WE HAVE PIZZA AND THEY TELL ME MAX IS GETTING HELP.

MAX WILL BE IN THE HOSPITAL FOR A FEW DAYS, HONEY. THERE ARE SPECIAL DOCTORS CALLED PSYCHIATRISTS THERE TO HELP HIM. THESE DOCTORS KNOW ALL ABOUT THE BRAIN AND WHAT MEDICINES CAN HELP THE BRAIN MOST.

THAT'S RIGHT. SOON, MAX WILL BE BACK HOME AND THINGS WILL BE BETTER.

I WANT TO KNOW MORE ABOUT MEDICINE. MRS. SMITH, MY TEACHER, TOLD ME I COULD MAKE A REPORT ABOUT IT IF I WANTED TO FOR SCHOOL. I READ AND READ, AND WENT ON THE INTERNET. FINALLY, I'M READY TO TALK ABOUT MY REPORT IN CLASS.

43

MY BROTHER MAX HAS AUTISM. IT'S HARD FOR HIM TO CONTROL HIS EMOTIONS OR TELL US HOW HE'S FEELING. HE ALSO HAS A HARD TIME WITH CHANGES. HE NEEDS MEDICINE BECAUSE HIS BRAIN WORKS DIFFERENTLY.

RESEARCHERS ARE DOCTORS THAT LOOK AT LOTS OF PLACES TO FIND THINGS THAT MAKE US BETTER. SOME MEDICINE COMES FROM PLANTS, AND SOME IS MADE BY PEOPLE.

RESEARCHERS MIX LOTS OF DIFFERENT INGREDIENTS TOGETHER TO MAKE MEDICINE. THEN, THEY TEST IT TO MAKE SURE IT WORKS.

WHEN A MEDICINE IS MADE, SPECIAL FACTORIES MAKE THOUSANDS AND THOUSANDS OF PILLS SO LOTS OF PEOPLE WHO NEED THE MEDICINE CAN GET IT. THE PILLS ARE MADE AT THE SPECIAL FACTORY, PUT IN BOXES, AND SENT TO DIFFERENT CITIES.

WHEN SOMEONE NEEDS MEDICINE, THEY GO TO A MEDICAL DOCTOR. THE DOCTOR KNOWS WHAT MEDICINE TO USE FOR SOMETHING LIKE AUTISM OR SOMETHING LIKE A STOMACH-ACHE. THEY PRESCRIBE THE MEDICINE, WHICH MEANS THEY GIVE A SPECIAL NOTE TO LET THE PHARMACY KNOW YOU CAN HAVE THE MEDICINE. THE PRESCRIPTION MAKES SURE YOU GET THE RIGHT MEDICINE.

AFTER YOU PICK UP MEDICINE AT THE PHARMACY, YOU HAVE TO LOOK OUT FOR SIDE EFFECTS. SIDE EFFECTS HAPPEN WHEN MEDICINE DOES SOMETHING YOU DON'T EXPECT. WHEN I GOT MEDICINE FOR STREP THROAT, MY MEDICINE GAVE ME A TUMMY ACHE. I WAS SURPRISED. SOMETIMES, BECAUSE OUR BODIES ARE ALL DIFFERENT, A MEDICINE DOES NOT WORK THE WAY IT SHOULD. A DOCTOR CAN GIVE YOU A DIFFERENT TYPE OF MEDICINE THAT MIGHT WORK BETTER.

YOU SHOULD NEVER TAKE MEDICINE THAT BELONGS TO SOMEBODY ELSE, NO MATTER WHAT. EVEN THOUGH MEDICINE IS TO HELP US, IT CAN HURT US IF WE DON'T TAKE IT THE RIGHT WAY. MEDICINE USUALLY MAKES US FEEL BETTER AND I HOPE IT MAKES MAX BETTER.

MAX COMES BACK FROM THE HOSPITAL. HE GIVES ME A SMILE AND SEEMS BETTER. HE TAKES HIS MEDICINE EVERY DAY.

MAX DOES NOT JUST GET MEDICINE. OTHER THINGS HAPPEN TO MAKE HIM BETTER. MAX HAS A NEW DOCTOR, A PSYCHIATRIST, THAT HE GOES TO SEE EVERY MONTH. MAX ALSO TALKS TO PEOPLE AT SCHOOL—PEOPLE CALLED COUNSELORS. THEY TALK TO HIM, PLAY GAMES WITH HIM AT A TABLE. THEY WORK WITH US, TOO, EXPLAINING HOW TO TALK WITH MAX AND WHAT TO DO IF HE GETS UPSET.

6:30	-Wake Up
6:30-7:00	-Bathroom / -Get Dressed
7:00-7:30	-Breakfast / -Medicine
7:30-3:00	-School
3:30-4:30	-Homework
4:30-6:00	-Video Games
6:	-Dinner

MAX IS MY BIG BROTHER.
HE IS FEELING BETTER NOW.

HE STILL HAS AUTISM
AND STILL GETS MAD
SOMETIMES, BUT MOST OF
THE TIME IT'S GOOD TO
SPEND TIME TOGETHER.

I HOPE THE MEDICINE HELPS HIM. MOM AND DAD SAY WE
HAVE TO WAIT AND SEE. WE MAY NEED TO DO OTHER
THINGS TO MAKE HIM BETTER.

AT HOME, I GET TO HELP MAX WHEN HE GETS UPSET.

IF HE GETS A LITTLE UPSET, HE LIKES IT WHEN WE HAND HIM A BALL TO SQUEEZE SO HE CAN FEEL BETTER.

IF HE GETS A LOT UPSET, I CAN GET MOM OR DAD SO THEY CAN GIVE PRESSURE AND HUGS TO HIS BODY SO HE FEELS SAFE AND HAPPIER.

TODAY, I DREW A PICTURE OF MY FAMILY FOR ART CLASS. I'M HAPPY MAX IS IN THE PICTURE AND IS SMILING. JUST LIKE THE REST OF US.

How These Books Were Created

The ORP Library of disabilities books is the result of heartfelt collaboration between numerous people: the staff of ORP, including the CEO, executive director, psychologists, clinical coordinators, teachers, and more; the families of children with disabilities served by ORP, including some of the children themselves; and the Round Table Companies (RTC) storytelling team. To create these books, RTC conducted dozens of intensive, intimate interviews over a period of months and performed independent research in order to truthfully and accurately depict the lives of these families. We are grateful to all those who donated their time in support of this message, generously sharing their experience, wisdom, and—most importantly—their stories so that the books will ring true. While each story is fictional and not based on any one family or child, we could not have envisioned the world through their eyes without the access we were so lovingly given. It is our hope that in reading this uniquely personal book, you felt the spirit of everyone who contributed to its creation.

Acknowledgments

Creating this comic book would not have been possible without the wisdom, patience, and experience of many generous individuals. In particular, the authors would like to thank retired Genesee Lake School health services director Karen Johnson and Genesee Lake School therapist Christy Lynch for providing valuable information and perspective on the realities and use of psychotropic medication with children. We would also like to thank Debbie Frisk, vice president of Oconomowoc Residential Programs, for her insights into day treatment programs, and Lorri Nelson, ORP executive assistant, for facilitating interviews, organizing material, and generally helping to wrangle the many moving parts that go into writing a book. Finally, we extend a heartfelt thank-you to E. L. Mendoza and the families who shared their journeys with autism spectrum disorder and psychotropic medications in such detail. This group of people was invaluable in bringing Justin's story to life, and the authors are deeply grateful.

Resources

for Families, Loved Ones, and Professionals

American Academy of Child and Adolescent Psychiatry
www.aacap.org

American Psychiatric Association
www.psychiatry.org

Mayo Clinic
www.mayoclinic.org

National Alliance on Mental Illness (NAMI)
www.nami.org

National Institute of Mental Health
www.nimh.nih.gov

Understanding Mental Disorders: Your Guide to DSM-5

University of Wisconsin Hospital and Clinics
www.uwhealth.org

Biographies

Nathan Lueth is a freelance illustrator and comic book artist currently residing in Saint Paul, MN. A 2004 graduate of the Minneapolis College of Art and Design, he has over 20 publication credits to his name, and continues to self-publish his own comic series, *Impure Blood*. He has seen first hand the way comics can change lives, and is proud to contribute his skills to the ORP Library. To see more of his work, you can view his portfolio at *www.nathanluethillustration.com*, or read his comic at *www.impurebloodwebcomic.com*.

Agata Antonow is a writer committed to book development, educational writing, and marketing. She discovered the power of reading early and has always wanted to share the magic of story with others. She graduated from McMaster University with a double honors major in history and English literature before embarking on graduate studies. Agata currently lives in Canada and is enthusiastic about being part of this ORP project.

James G. Balestrieri is currently the CEO of Oconomowoc Residential Programs, Inc. (ORP). He has worked in the human services field for over 40 years, gaining experience in nearly every area. With a passion for creatively addressing the needs of those with impairments by managing the inherent stress among funding, programming, and profitability, Jim believes that people with disabilities have a right to find their place in the world and to achieve their maximum potential as individuals. For more information, see *www.orp.com*.

Jeffrey D. Krukar, Ph.D. is a licensed psychologist and certified school psychologist with more than 20 years of experience working with children and families in a variety of settings. As the psychologist at Genesee Lake School in Oconomowoc, WI, Dr. Krukar hopes the ORP Library of disabilities books will bring stories of children and families to a world that is generally not aware of their challenges and successes, as well as offer a sense of hope to those currently on this journey.

Nicolette E. Weisensel, M.D., F.A.P.A., is a board-certified psychiatrist who has experience in a variety of practice settings including outpatient, inpatient, residential, and day treatment and expertise in the treatment of eating disorders. Dr. Weisensel earned her M.D. from the University of Wisconsin School of Medicine and Public Health. She also completed her psychiatry residency at the University of Wisconsin, serving as chief resident during her final year. She has presented on a variety of topics at regional, national, and international conferences regarding eating disorders.

Katie Gutierrez holds a BA in English and philosophy from Southwestern University and an MFA in fiction from Texas State University. Since 2007, she has edited upwards of 75 books and co-written 10, including several in the ORP medication series. She has been humbled by the stories she has heard and hopes these books will help guide families on their journeys, connecting them with valuable resources and support.

About ORP

Oconomowoc Residential Programs, Inc. is an employee-owned family of companies making a difference in the lives of people with disabilities. With service locations throughout Wisconsin and Indiana, our dedicated staff of 2,400 people provides quality services and professional care to more than 1,950 children, adolescents, and adults with special needs. ORP provides a comprehensive continuum of care. Child and adolescent programs include developmentally appropriate education and treatment in settings specifically attuned to their needs. These include residential therapeutic education and vocational services for students from all around the country. For those in or near Wisconsin and Indiana, we offer community-based residential supports, in-home supports, in- and out-of-home respite care, and alternative therapeutic day-school programs. We provide special programs for students with specific academic and social issues relative to a wide range of complex disabilities, including autism spectrum disorders, Asperger's disorder, cognitive and developmental disabilities, anxiety disorders, depression, bipolar disorder, reactive attachment disorder, attention deficit disorder, severe emotional and behavioral issues, Prader-Willi syndrome, and other impairments. Our adult services continuum includes community-based residential services for people with intellectual, developmental, and physical disabilities, brain injury, mental health and other behavioral impairments, and the medically fragile. We also provide independent living homes, supervised apartments, community-based supports for adults in mental health crisis, day service programs, and respite services.

At ORP, our guiding principle is passion: a passion for the people we serve and for the work we do.

For a comprehensive look at each of our programs, please visit *www.orp.com*. For a collection of resources for parents, educators and administrators, and healthcare professionals who are raising or supporting children with disabilities, please visit the ORP Library at *www.orplibrary.com*.

PSYCHOTROPIC MEDICATION

Medicine for My Big Brother is an adaptation of *Connecting with Max*, the second of three books in the ORP Library focusing on the use of psychotropic medication in children and adolescents. The medication series includes *Connecting with Max*, *Finding Balance*, and *Can I Go Home with You?* Based on dozens of interviews with parents and clinicians, each book explores challenges with side effects, treatment adherence, and dosage and medication changes; highlights successes and explains the importance of a comprehensive biopsychosocial treatment plan; and aims to educate families, caregivers, and healthcare professionals on the short-term and long-term impact of including psychotropic medication in a child's treatment plan.

ASPERGER'S DISORDER

Meltdown and its companion comic book, *Melting Down*, are both based on the fictional story of Benjamin, a boy diagnosed with Asperger's disorder and additional challenging behavior. From the time Benjamin is a toddler, he and his parents know he is different: he doesn't play with his sister, refuses to make eye contact, and doesn't communicate well with others. And his tantrums are not like normal tantrums; they're meltdowns that will eventually make regular schooling—and day-to-day life—impossible. Both the prose book, intended for parents, educators, and mental health professionals, and the comic for the kids themselves demonstrate that the journey toward hope isn't simple . . . but with the right tools and teammates, it's possible.

AUTISM SPECTRUM DISORDER

Mr. Incredible shares the fictional story of Adam, a boy diagnosed with autistic disorder. On Adam's first birthday, his mother recognizes that something is different about him: he recoils from the touch of his family, preferring to accept physical contact only in the cool water of the family's pool. As Adam grows older, he avoids eye contact, is largely nonverbal, and has very specific ways of getting through the day; when those habits are disrupted, intense meltdowns and self-harmful behavior follow. From seeking a diagnosis to advocating for special education services, from keeping Adam safe to discovering his strengths, his family becomes his biggest champion. The journey to realizing Adam's potential isn't easy, but with hope, love, and the right tools and teammates, they find that Adam truly is *Mr. Incredible*. The companion comic in this series, inspired by social stories, offers an innovative, dynamic way to guide children—and parents, educators, and caregivers—through some of the daily struggles experienced by those with autism.

BULLYING

Nearly one third of all school children face physical, verbal, social, or cyber bullying on a regular basis. Educators and parents search for ways to end bullying, but as that behavior becomes more sophisticated, it's harder to recognize and stop. In *Classroom Heroes*, Jason is a quiet, socially awkward seventh grader who has long suffered bullying in silence. His parents notice him becoming angrier and more withdrawn, but they don't realize the scope of the problem until one bully takes it too far—and one teacher acts on her determination to stop it. Both *Classroom Heroes* and *How to Be a Hero*—along with a supporting coloring book (*Heroes in the Classroom*) and curriculum guide (*Those Who Bully and Those Who Are Bullied*)—recognize that stopping bullying requires a change in mindset: adults and children must create a community that simply does not tolerate bullying. These books provide practical yet very effective strategies to end bullying, one student at a time.

FAMILY SUPPORT

Schuyler Walker was just four years old when he was diagnosed with autism, bipolar disorder, and ADHD. In 2004, childhood mental illness was rarely talked about or understood. With knowledge and resources scarce, Schuyler's mom, Christine, navigated a lonely maze to determine what treatments, medications, and therapies could benefit her son. In the ten years since his diagnosis, Christine has often wished she had a "how to" guide that would provide the real mom-to-mom information she needed to survive the day and, in the end, help her family navigate the maze with knowledge, humor, grace, and love. Christine may not have had a manual at the beginning of her journey, but she hopes this book will serve as yours.

PRADER-WILLI SYNDROME

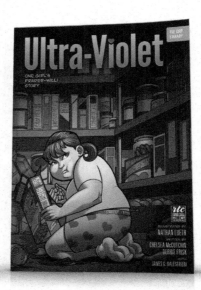

Estimated to occur once in every 15,000 births, Prader-Willi syndrome is a rare genetic disorder that includes features of cognitive disabilities, problem behaviors, and, most pervasively, chronic hunger that leads to dangerous overeating and its life-threatening consequences. *Insatiable: A Prader-Willi Story* and its companion comic book, *Ultra-Violet: One Girl's Prader-Willi Story*, draw on dozens of intensive interviews to offer insight into the world of those struggling with Prader-Willi syndrome. Both books tell the fictional story of Violet, a vivacious young girl born with the disorder, and her family, who—with the help of experts—will not give up their quest to give her a healthy and happy life.

REACTIVE ATTACHMENT DISORDER

An Unlikely Trust: Alina's Story of Adoption, Complex Trauma, Healing, and Hope, and its companion children's book, *Alina's Story*, share the journey of Alina, a young girl adopted from Russia. After living in an orphanage during her early life, Alina is unequipped to cope with the complexities of the outside world. She has a deep mistrust of others and finds it difficult to talk about her feelings. When she is frightened, overwhelmed, or confused, she lashes out in rages that scare her family. Alina's parents know she needs help and work endlessly to find it for her, eventually discovering a special school that will teach Alina new skills. Slowly, Alina gets better at expressing her feelings and solving problems. For the first time in her life, she realizes she is truly safe and loved . . . and capable of loving in return.

CPSIA information can be obtained
at www.ICGtesting.com
Printed in the USA
LVOW06s0802290816

501992LV00001B/1/P